EXPLORING
ANCIENT CHINA

by Pamela Herron

www.12StoryLibrary.com

12-Story Library is an imprint of Bookstaves and Press Room Editions

Produced for 12-Story Library by Red Line Editorial

Photographs ©: jhphoto/Imaginechina/AP Images, cover, 1; Los Angeles County Museum of Art, 4, 15, 24, 28; Fine Art Images/Heritage Images/Hulton Archive/Getty Images, 5; cl2004lhy/Shutterstock Images, 6; typhoonski/iStockphoto, 7; Nils Jorgensen/Rex Features/AP Images, 9; Mathisa/ Shutterstock Images, 8; Zhao jian kang/Shutterstock Images, 10; beibaoke/Shutterstock, 11; Valmol48/iStockphoto, 12, 29; William Randolph Hearst Collection/Los Angeles County Museum of Art, 13; pidjoe/iStockphoto, 14; Vassil, 16; tandem/Shutterstock, 17; Mu jun/Imaginechina/AP Images, 18; Wolfgang Kaehler/Superstock/Glow Images, 19, 22; Werner Forman Archive/Heritage Images/Glow Images, 20; Zhang Peng/LightRocket/Getty Images, 21; CM Dixon/Print Collector/Hulton Archive/Getty Images, 23; Superstock/Glow Images, 25; SeanPavonePhoto/iStockphoto, 26; loonger/iStockphoto, 27

Content Consultant: Sarah A. Queen, Professor of History, Connecticut College

Library of Congress Cataloging-in-Publication Data
Names: Herron, Pamela, author.
Title: Exploring ancient China / by Pamela Herron.
Description: Mankato, MN : 12-Story Library, [2018] | Series: Exploring
  ancient civilizations | Audience: Grades 4 to 6. | Includes
  bibliographical references and index.
Identifiers: LCCN 2016052222 (print) | LCCN 2016057747 (ebook) | ISBN
  9781632354617 (hardcover : alkaline paper) | ISBN 9781632355263 (paperback:
  alkaline paper) | ISBN 9781621435785 (hosted e-book)
Subjects: LCSH: China--Civilization--To 221 B.C.--Juvenile literature. |
  China--Civilization--221 B.C.-960 A.D.--Juvenile literature. |
  China--Civilization--960-1644--Juvenile literature.
Classification: LCC DS721 .H4992 2018 (print) | LCC DS721 (ebook) | DDC
  951--dc23
LC record available at https://lccn.loc.gov/2016052222

Printed in the United States of America
022017

Access free, up-to-date content on this topic plus a full digital version of this book. Scan the QR code on page 31 or use your school's login at 12StoryLibrary.com.

Table of Contents

China Is One of the Oldest Civilizations

China is a large country in Asia. It is slightly bigger than the United States. China is home to one of the longest-lasting civilizations in the world. For more than 5,000 years, the people of China have grown crops, built huge monuments, and made scientific discoveries. Fireworks, gunpowder, paper, and the compass can all be traced back to ancient China.

Historians divide ancient China into time periods called dynasties. A dynasty is a line of several rulers who come from the same family or group of people. When a ruler from a new family came to power, this created a new dynasty. Most dynasties lasted approximately

300 years. Corrupt or conquered rulers paved the way for a new emperor. The first dynasty was the Xia. It lasted from approximately 2070 to 1600 BCE.

No written records survive from the earliest emperors and their dynasties. There is little archaeological evidence. People wrote about the first dynasties centuries after they happened. These stories are partially or mostly mythical. Tales about the earliest emperors, such as the Yellow Emperor, are legends. These emperors get credit for inventing important parts of Chinese culture, such as writing and making silk cloth.

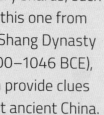

Pottery shards, such as this one from the Shang Dynasty (1600–1046 BCE), can provide clues about ancient China.

QIN DYNASTY RULE

Shih Huangdi's rule was strict and controlling. He standardized writing and measurements. He built highways and fortresses. He took land away from the local lords who had ruled before. Instead, he ordered government officials to supervise each area. He ordered books burned and intellectuals killed if they went against his policies. And he raised taxes. After his death, the people rebelled. The Qin dynasty ended. But many of the changes he made remained.

姓嬴名政始自始皇乙卯即王位庚辰併天下稱皇帝
在位三十七年居王位二十五年即帝位十二年壽五十

A later artist imagines Emperor Shih Huangdi.

15
Approximate number of years the Qin Dynasty lasted.

- People have lived in China for more than 5,000 years.
- Historians divide ancient China into dynasties.
- Little evidence exists from the earliest dynasties and emperors.
- China became a unified territory during the Qin Dynasty.

China did not exist as a unified empire until the 200s BCE. The city-state of Qin (pronounced "Chin") conquered smaller city-states. This brought a large area under one government. The leader of Qin, Ying Zheng, ruled this area from 221 to 207 BCE. He created a new title for himself, Shih Huangdi, or "First Emperor." This era is also known as the Qin Dynasty.

2

The Government of China Was Based on Morals

The Qin Dynasty fell in 206 BCE. Afterward, the Han Dynasty came to power until 220 CE. Literature and art flourished during the Han Dynasty. The government under Han emperors was based on the teachings of the philosopher Confucius (551–479 BCE). The empire was divided into several areas. Each area had its own set of rulers, sent by the central government. Local officials reported to the rulers in each province. These rulers reported back to the advisers to the emperor.

Many laws in ancient China were about morals. The laws set limits on how people of different classes should interact

with one another. Government officials enforced the laws and fined or punished lawbreakers. They also collected taxes and kept records.

Under the Han Dynasty, people with good morals were rewarded. Government officials with good morals were promoted. These workers demonstrated their knowledge of Confucius and his teachings through a series of exams. Education was a high priority in

These bronze coins were made during the Han Dynasty.

ancient China. Students would study for years preparing for the exams. They began at the local level. Successful candidates moved up to eventually take regional and national exams. This system based on knowledge and study was the basis for ancient Chinese government for over 2,000 years.

250,000
Population of the Han capital city, Chang'an, in 2 CE.

- The Han Dynasty began in 206 BCE.
- The empire was divided into administrative areas.
- Government officials took tests based on Confucian texts.

CONFUCIUS (551–479 BCE)

Confucius is the most famous and important ancient Chinese philosopher and teacher. His real name was Kong Qui. In Chinese, he is called Kongzi or Kongfuzi, which means "Master Kong." He believed it was important to be honorable and respect your ancestors. His legacy includes the Five Classics, or Wujing. These five texts influenced Chinese government and culture for thousands of years.

Confucius is always shown with a beard.

3

The Ancient Chinese Practiced More Than One Religion

China has never had just one religion. Since before the first dynasty, people have worshipped family ancestors, nature, and forces such as good luck. Honoring ghosts and the dead remains important to this day.

For almost 2,000 years, people have practiced Confucianism in China. Followers of Confucius wrote down his teachings in a book called the *Analects*. But his ideas were not new. Confucius spread ideas of virtue and respect for one's ancestors.

Confucianism teaches that individuals must be moral. That way, they will live in harmony with the universe. Rulers and teachers must live the right way so others will follow them.

Another common belief system of the time was "the Dao" or the Way. The Dao is a force of the universe that flows through everything and ties it together. The *Daodejing* is a book that explains the important parts of Daoism. Legend says it was written by a scholar named Laozi.

Daoist temple in Guangdong, Guangzhou

Some say Laozi met Confucius before his death. Historians now think the *Daodejing* was written by many people.

In approximately 100 CE, Buddhist monks made their way from India to China. Buddhists believe that the source of suffering is desire. Chinese scholars translated Buddhist texts, called *sutras*. Buddhist temples and statues were built all over China. Things changed in 845 CE. At the time, it was against the law to collect taxes from Buddhist temples. But the government needed money. So it closed more than 4,000 temples and took control of millions of acres of land. Afterward, Buddhism was still practiced in China, but the formal Buddhist church was never as powerful as it once was.

51,000
Number of Buddhist images in the Yun'gang Buddhist Caves near Datong, China.

- Ancient Chinese people worshipped nature, their ancestors, and forces such as good luck.
- Confucianism, Daoism, and Buddhism were all important religions in ancient China.
- Each religion teaches people how to live a good life.
- Buddhism grew less powerful after 845 CE.

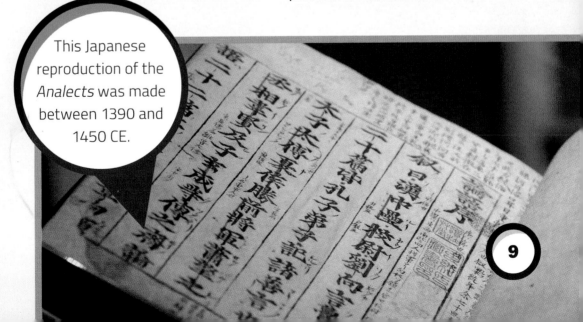

This Japanese reproduction of the *Analects* was made between 1390 and 1450 CE.

4

The Ancient Chinese Built Famous Structures

The most famous structure in China is the Great Wall of China. It is the longest wall on earth. Building began in the Qin Dynasty under Shih Huangdi. He ordered laborers in the north to construct a huge wall to help defend the empire. They also connected sections of older, shorter walls. Legend says that more than one million workers died during construction of the original wall.

A remarkable engineering achievement was the Grand Canal. It was built during the Sui Dynasty. In 605 CE, laborers dug a canal almost 1,200 miles (1,931 km) long.

The Grand Canal connected northern cities with the Yangzi River. This was important for trade and transportation. Relay and military posts established along the way helped secure this vast territory.

Feng shui has influenced Chinese architecture for thousands of years. The term means "wind water." Feng shui is connected to Daoist beliefs about living in harmony with nature. Feng shui experts were consulted before ancient cities and homes were built. They considered

The majority of the Great Wall still standing today is from the Ming Dynasty (1368–1644).

compass point directions, the location of mountains and water, and the most harmonious flow of energy. Mountains and rivers are sacred in China and believed to have excellent feng shui.

Most ancient Chinese homes were built out of wood. Homes of the wealthy were several stories high. To protect these wooden houses, rammed earth walls were built to surround cities. These walls were created by compacting mud until it was several inches thick. Rammed earth was also used in building the Great Wall.

The mountains behind the Songyue Pagoda means it has good feng shui.

FENG SHUI

Buildings with good feng shui usually face south and have a water feature nearby. It is best to have mountains behind for protection. Many of the ideas behind feng shui are based on common sense about weather and landforms. Today, all over the world, people study to become feng shui experts.

13,171
Length, in miles (21,197 km), of the Great Wall.

- Work on the Great Wall of China began during the Qin Dynasty.
- The Grand Canal was dug during the Sui Dynasty to connect cities with the Yangzi River.
- Ancient builders followed the principles of feng shui so their buildings would be in harmony with nature.
- Rammed earth walls protected cities.

11

5

Ceremonies and Grave Goods Protected People in the Afterlife

In ancient China, ancestors were especially important. Most families had a temple or shrine to house carved stones representing their ancestors. The ancient Chinese believed their ancestors who died were still close to them. These ancestors are celebrated during the festival of *Qing Ming*. The term means "clear brightness" and is known as tomb sweeping day in English. Qing Ming is similar to Memorial Day in the United States. People visit family cemeteries to clean gravestones, pray, burn incense, and bring offerings to honor their dead ancestors. Celebrating the festival of Qing Ming started before the Qin Dynasty began.

Emperors built elaborate tombs so they would be comfortable in the afterlife. Farmers digging a well in 1974 first discovered the tomb of Shih Huangdi near the city of Xi'an. The tomb was filled with

Parts of Shih Huangdi's terra-cotta army have been displayed in museums around the world.

THINK ABOUT IT

People in other ancient cultures, such as Egyptians, also left items in tombs for the dead to use in the afterlife. What physical items are most important to you? Why?

This sculpture of a camel was buried with someone who died during the Tang Dynasty.

thousands of life-size terra-cotta warriors, horses, and chariots. These brownish-orange clay soldiers, chariots, and horses were meant to guard the emperor.

8,000

Estimated number of terra-cotta warriors in Shih Huangdi's tomb.

- The ancient Chinese held festivals to honor family ancestors.
- Emperors created elaborate tombs with items they would need for the afterlife.
- Common people were buried with grave goods, too.

Most ancient royal tombs were looted long ago. Some royal tombs from the Han Dynasty survived in eastern China. These tombs look like palaces. Grave goods included everything needed in the afterlife, such as musical instruments, weapons, and cookware.

Common people were also buried with favorite tools, food, and other items believed to help them. Grave goods from the Han Dynasty were often models of things from everyday life. They include houses, animals, and other objects.

6

Rice, Wheat, Tea, and Silk Were Important to Trade

Food in ancient China reflected the diversity of the people living there and the different geographic regions. People grew rice only in valleys in the south with rich soil. Areas in the north relied much more on wheat or millet. Northern people ate mostly noodles or buns made from flour. Most dishes used small amounts of meat with vegetables and sauces.

In ancient China, tea was used for rituals or for medicine. By the 600s CE, tea became popular as a social drink to enjoy with friends and family. Influential families often had special cups and pots designed just for them. Some pottery makers produced tea sets for the imperial family only.

The ancient Chinese discovered how to make silk. Silk clothing was expensive. Only royalty and high-ranking families could afford it. Common Chinese people were not allowed to wear it at all. Most people wore clothing made of hemp, a plant with tough fibers. Emperors also gave silk goods as gifts to other rulers. Artisans made paintings on silk canvases.

The tea crop is still important in China today.

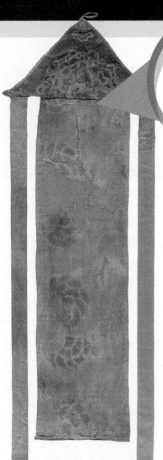

Silk banner from the Tang Dynasty

THINK ABOUT IT

Tea was once considered so valuable that people would lock it up to keep it safe. Today, tea is inexpensive and can easily be purchased from the grocery store. Why do some goods lose their value over time? Why do some things, such as gold, remain precious?

China's Silk Road wasn't really a road at all but a series of trade routes. The Silk Road got its name from foreign traders. People from the Middle East, Europe, Africa, and other parts of Asia all traveled to China. They wanted to trade goods for China's beautiful silk fabrics, their delicious tea, and more. During the Tang Dynasty, the capital city Chang'an was a busy trade center. On any day in Chang'an, dozens of different languages might be spoken as people traded goods and ideas.

1,583
Number of years the Silk Road was used heavily (130 BCE–1453 CE).

- Food in ancient China varied in the north and south.
- Tea was important socially as well as for medicine and rituals.
- Silk clothing was expensive and worn only by royalty in ancient China.
- Silk was one of many goods traded with the West through the Silk Road trade network.

7

Ancient Chinese Families Lived Together

In ancient China, many people lived together in small villages and often farmed land together. Most homes held several generations of a family. Once a wealthier family owned land, they would build their first house. As the family grew, they built additional rooms for the sons, creating a large family compound. Grandparents, uncles, aunts, nieces, and nephews might all live within the same compound.

Many villages had a large public square. People gathered there for celebrations, music, dancing, and special events. Some villages also had theaters or temples. Local officials lived in the villages or cities

they governed. Many cities had walls for protection.

Social class was usually decided at birth. Children belonged to the same social class as their parents. Children of peasants grew up to be peasants. Children of the nobility grew up to be nobles. The middle classes included merchants and government workers. One way to move up in society was to pass the civil service exams. But it was difficult for a peasant child to get an education.

This Chinese shoe was designed for a bound foot.

Women were not considered equal to men. The family name and property passed to sons, not daughters. Men could have multiple wives, called concubines. They could divorce their wives, but women could not divorce their husbands. Most women were not allowed to work outside the home. The ancient Chinese also practiced foot binding. This painful procedure broke a young girl's toes under her feet, making it hard for her to walk or work for the rest of her life. It was believed to be a symbol of beauty.

1,859
Number of cities in 754 CE during the Tang Dynasty.

- Many ancient Chinese people lived in villages.
- Several generations of wealthier families often lived together in one house.
- Children were born into the same social class as their parents.
- Women did not have the same opportunities as men in ancient China.

Standing chopsticks up in a bowl of rice is considered bad manners.

HISTORY OF CHOPSTICKS

Chopsticks have been used in China for about 5,000 years. The first chopsticks were probably twigs used to stir or pick up food from cooking pots. In ancient China, emperors sometimes used silver chopsticks. They believed the silver would turn black if the chopsticks touched poisoned food.

Chinese Writing Has a Long History

The Chinese language does not have an alphabet. Instead each Chinese character is a picture, or symbol. Symbols show concepts or ideas. Scholars can read ancient documents because Chinese characters have not changed too much over 3,000 years.

Chinese is one of the oldest written languages in the world still in use. Some scholars believe it has a history going back 6,000 years. The pictographs have changed over time. But they still represent the same concepts or ideas.

Some of the earliest written characters are on the "oracle bones" from the Shang Dynasty (1600–1046 BCE). These are ox shoulder bones or turtle shells. People wrote symbols on them and used them to try to tell the future. Written Chinese language was standardized under Emperor Qin. After that, most people in ancient China read and wrote the same characters. However, the way Chinese was spoken varied from region to region. For example, in parts of northern China they spoke Mandarin. In parts of the south, they spoke Cantonese. This is still true today, but Mandarin is the official language.

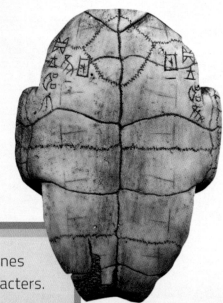

The Shang Dynasty oracle bones show early written Chinese characters.

A painting from the Tang Dynasty

Painting, poetry, and music are important parts of Chinese culture. China is home to some of the earliest books and many precious works of art made of bronze and jade. The *Book of Songs* is the oldest existing collection of Chinese poetry. It contains 305 poems that date from the 1000s to the 600s BCE.

105 CE
Year true paper is invented, replacing bamboo scrolls.

- Chinese writing does not have an alphabet.
- Each symbol shows a concept or an idea.
- The Shang Dynasty oracle bones have some of the earliest written characters.
- Poetry and art are important in Chinese culture.

SEALS AND CHOPS

For more than 3,000 years, Chinese people have used a seal to sign their names. It is sometimes called a chop instead. Seals were carved with a family's name and usually made of stone. When a document needed a signature, it was typically stamped in red ink with the seal. Emperor Qin was the first ruler to begin using the seal for official signatures. Seals were used for debts, buying or selling property, and government business.

Ancient Chinese Inventions Changed the World

Many inventions first created in China are still used today. Paper was invented in 105 CE. The ancient Chinese also made books by painting characters on bamboo strips. Chinese monks invented woodblock printing during the Tang Dynasty. The oldest surviving printed book with a date is the *Diamond Sutra*. It's a Buddhist text that was translated into Chinese and printed in 868 CE.

In China, people have celebrated with fireworks for about 1,000 years. The earliest fireworks date back to about 200 BCE. They were pieces of bamboo that exploded when thrown into a fire. Many years later, people experimented by adding other ingredients, such as iron shavings and gunpowder. Chinese

The text and pictures of the *Diamond Sutra* were carved in wood, coated in ink, and pressed onto paper.

The fish's mouth in this compass will point south when the bowl is filled with water.

alchemists invented gunpowder by accident during the Tang Dynasty. They experimented with many substances while trying to develop a way to live forever. During the

Song Dynasty (960–1279 CE), people began using gunpowder bombs and flares in warfare.

As early as the Qin Dynasty, people used a compass to determine the best time and place for burials. They used magnetic ore, a type of iron. They knew it would always point in a north-south direction. Feng shui experts used the compass to site buildings. By 1000 CE, sailors used magnetized needles to travel across oceans. Evidence suggests that Europe learned about the compass from China. Many other inventions began in China and were later shared or traded with other nations.

17

Length, in feet (5 m), of the *Diamond Sutra*, a book printed on a long roll of paper.

- The ancient Chinese invented paper and woodblock printing.
- They invented fireworks and gunpowder.
- They used compasses for burials and to follow the principles of feng shui.

Ancient China Was Shaped by War

In early China, lords of small states fought with one another to rule the land. They used bronze weapons and tools by the 2000s BCE. The first kings and then later emperors were leaders who managed to unite larger areas under their control.

The ancient Chinese also had to fight outside invaders. Many bands of warriors came from Central Asia.

GIANT ANCIENT ARMIES

From 475 to 221 BCE, armies became more organized. They included peasant soldiers, archers, and cavalry. The warring states gathered large armies with up to 200,000 men each. By the Qin Dynasty, professional soldiers replaced peasants.

A Tang Dynasty tomb painting shows soldiers riding to war.

By 1700 BCE, these invaders had wheeled chariots and horses. The Chinese quickly adopted the chariot and used a powerful bow.

Around the time of Confucius *The Art of War* was written. Master Sun is traditionally listed as the book's author. He is also called Sunzi or Sun Tzu. He wrote at a time when many Chinese regions competed with one another for

1972

Year the most complete version of *The Art of War* was discovered in Shandong Province in China.

- Small states warred with one another.
- The ancient Chinese had to fight invaders, but they also learned new military inventions from them.
- *The Art of War* advised leaders on strategy and warfare.

control. From 722–221 BCE, many small states fought to conquer or overthrow one another. *The Art of War* talks about battle strategies. More importantly, the book talks about whether a war or battle should even be fought at all. Leaders were encouraged to consider the impact of war on their people. The book says the goal of war is not honor or glory, but victory. This book has remained important throughout China and the rest of the world.

Pottery model of an ancient Chinese watchtower

The Ancient Chinese Empire Fell . . . and Rose Again

During the Song Dynasty, people made advances in farming and industry. Rice growing expanded in the south. The production of silk, porcelain, and ceramics was perfected. Book making and paper making were more popular than ever. Trade increased so rapidly that the government printed paper money for the first time. Metal coins weighed too much to be carried easily. All of this economic growth in peaceful times led to many people living outside city walls. People were not just focused on trade and manufacturing. Much like the Tang Dynasty, this was a time of poetry, painting, and writing. Even the emperor, Huizong, was interested in the arts. He was not a great

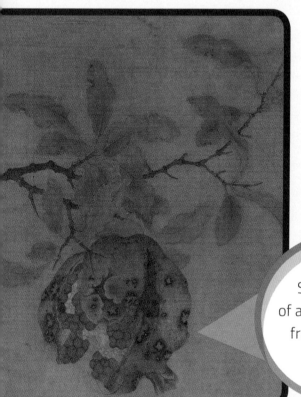

Silk painting of a pomegranate from the Song Dynasty

leader, though. He built expensive gardens and put the government in debt.

Jurchen warriors from Manchuria in northern China invaded. The Song emperor moved the capital to the city of Hangzhou in the south. But the country was weakened. In the 1200s CE, China eventually fell to the Mongols, also from the north. Chinese culture was so influential that even foreign conquerors such as the Mongols adapted their ways. Foreigners eventually became more like the Chinese rather than making them adapt to a new culture.

100 million

Number of people who lived in China by the mid-Song period.

- Chinese culture flourished during the Song Dynasty.
- Jurchen warriors conquered the north.
- The Mongols conquered the rest of China in the 1200s CE.

Genghis Khan, leader of the Mongols, began the conquest of China.

KAIFENG PAINTING

One of China's most well-known paintings is from the Song Dynasty. This painting shows the city of Kaifeng. It was the Song capital before the Jurchen conquest. It is alive with views of travelers, merchants and shopkeepers, ships, bridges, and street scenes. The details have been studied for centuries by scholars wanting to learn about everyday life during the Song era.

Ancient China Gave the World Many Gifts

Many qualities of Chinese culture strongly influenced surrounding countries. Chinese language, literature, and philosophy have had a lasting impact on all of Asia and continue to do so today. Inventions such as gunpowder and the compass changed warfare and how people navigate. It is impossible to measure the effects of both on world history. Writing, paper, printing, and silk were key developments that also spread beyond China's borders.

In ancient times, China was a powerful country. Its culture had a large effect, especially on neighboring countries. Places such as Japan, Korea, Vietnam, and

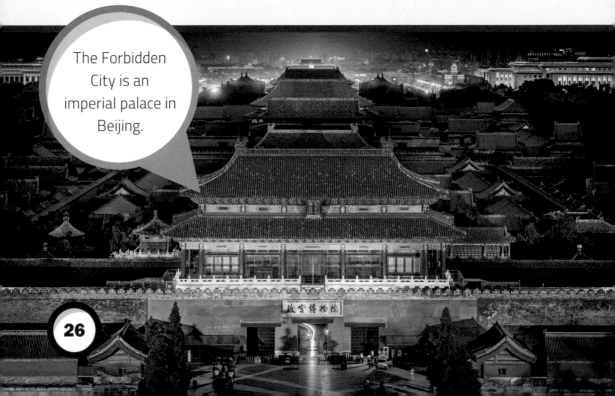

The Forbidden City is an imperial palace in Beijing.

Celebrations such as the Chinese New Year keep ancient traditions alive.

others looked to China for the best literature, music, painting, and fashion. In ancient times, educated people from these other countries learned to read and write in Chinese. Chinese philosophy continues to have an important effect on society and culture around the world.

The ancient Chinese government, based on promoting people with good morals, allowed the empire to flourish. This idea of rewarding people based on their merits survives today. Archaeological finds show what life was like for those who lived long ago.

1912
Year the last emperor of China gave up his throne.

- Chinese inventions, including gunpowder, the compass, paper, and silk, spread worldwide.
- Chinese culture had a large impact on the rest of Asia in ancient times that continues today.
- Literature and art from ancient China teach us today about life in the past.

12 Key Dates

2070–1600 BCE
The first dynasty, the Xia, rules ancient China.

1600–1046 BCE
The Shang Dynasty rules China; the earliest written Chinese characters are carved on the oracle bones.

1000s–600s BCE
Poems in the *Book of Songs* are composed.

722–221 BCE
Many Chinese states fight with one another for power and control; *The Art of War* is written during this time.

551–479 BCE
Confucius practices philosophy; his teachings influence Chinese government and religion for thousands of years.

221 BCE
Shih Huangdi comes to power and creates the Qin Dynasty; construction on the Great Wall begins.

206 BCE to 220 CE
The Han Dynasty rules China.

200s BCE
Early fireworks made out of bamboo are created.

130 BCE to 1453 CE
Silk Road routes are heavily used for trade.

105 CE
Paper is invented, replacing earlier bamboo scrolls.

1279 CE
The Song Dynasty ends and ancient China falls to the Mongols after the capital city is captured.

1974 CE
Farmers find the tomb of Shih Huangdi and the army of terra-cotta soldiers.

Glossary

alchemist
A person who uses an unscientific process to try to turn metal into gold, develop a cure for all diseases, or discover a means for immortality.

ancestor
A member of one's family who lived a long time ago.

cemetery
A field where dead people are buried.

culture
The habits and beliefs of a particular group of people.

elaborate
Done with great care or having many details.

fortress
A place built to withstand attacks.

influential
Having a powerful effect.

invader
A person who enters another land to try to take it over.

legacy
Something that comes from the past and is handed down by each generation.

literature
Written works that are valued for a long period of time.

philosophy
The study of knowledge, reality, and morals.

ritual
An event that is repeated the same way, year after year.

For More Information

Books

Lonely Planet. *Not-for-Parents China: Everything You Ever Wanted to Know*. Oakland, CA: Lonely Planet, 2012.

Ransom, Candice. *Tools and Treasures of Ancient China*. Minneapolis, MN: Lerner, 2014.

Stanborough, Rebecca. *The Great Wall of China*. North Mankato, MN: Capstone Press, 2016.

Visit 12StoryLibrary.com

Scan the code or use your school's login at **12StoryLibrary.com** for recent updates about this topic and a full digital version of this book. Enjoy free access to:

- Digital ebook
- Breaking news updates
- Live content feeds
- Videos, interactive maps, and graphics
- Additional web resources

Note to educators: Visit 12StoryLibrary.com/register to sign up for free premium website access. Enjoy live content plus a full digital version of every 12-Story Library book you own for every student at your school.

Index

About the Author
Pamela Herron is a poet and writer who teaches Chinese culture, Confucianism, and Daoism for the University of Texas at El Paso. She enjoys spending time with her Chinese American family scattered over the United States, Canada, China, and Hong Kong.